GRANDFATHER
STORIES

Enjoy

GRANDFATHER STORIES

THE FAMILY FARM OF THE 1930'S AND 40'S

Perry Treadwell

Writer's Showcase
presented by *Writer's Digest*
San Jose New York Lincoln Shanghai

Grandfather Stories
The Family Farm of the 1930's and 40's

Writer's Showcase
presented by *Writer's Digest*
an imprint of iUniverse.com, Inc.

For information address:
iUniverse.com, Inc.
5220 S 16th, Ste. 200
Lincoln, NE 68512
www.iuniverse.com

ISBN: 0-595-00087-8

Printed in the United States of America

*Dedicated to my granddaughters Sarah Elise Thompson,
Amanda Lynn Treadwell and Amy Treadwell Clower.*

Contents

Introduction

I began writing stories about my experiences on my grandparents' farm for my granddaughters during the1980s. Rereading them a decade later I realized that they are more than children's stories. With the turn of this century much of the history of the small family farm will be forgotten. Here are my memories of growing up on a working farm of the 1930s and 40s. The sights, sounds and smells of a pre-World War II farm are quite different from the modern industrial farm. I had the opportunity to work with horses, milk-cows, pigs, sheep, and chickens on the same section of land. Dogs called Shep or Billy came and went. Cats followed Grandad from the barn with his two pails of milk. Chickens fussed and squawked and produced eggs that had to be collected every evening. Nights hardly cooled from the heat of the day. Rotating fans served as the only air conditioning after electricity came. Heat lightning walked across the slate sky. The kitchen smelled of wood-fire, fresh peach or cherry cobbler, and churned butter. On the back porch where the work boots and the straw hats resided, the slop bucket full of old milk gave off its sourer odor to mix with odors of kerosene and mud. There were chamber pots under the bed for night time use rather than trekking to the outhouse. Long-legged calves with runny behinds bawled for their moms during the day.

Family Origins

This farm, located in Gentry County, Missouri, was part of a farm culture brought to this country by the yeomanry of the British Isles.

Bagpipes. The skirl of bagpipes prickles the back of my neck and catches my breath. Is there some script in my DNA which twists and turns certain nerve paths whenever that squeal is heard? I am the product of the ebb and flow of the great waves of immigration which washed across the American landscape. My chromosomes contain a genetic soup of Scotch, Irish, Welch and English genes savored with a pinch of French garlic. In the mid 19th century, these genes flowed into Gentry County to establish a quiet pool of farmers.

My maternal grandmother's roots originate in the cold mists of Norway sometime in the 9th century. These "Norsemen" left their homes to raid, then populate, the warm land of the Normandy peninsula. The Pattonnes of France became the great Patton clan first as Scottish nobles and Presbyterians in the 16th century and then as Irish immigrants to William Penn's experiment in the 18th century.

When the English did not extend the Toleration Act of 1698 to Ireland, only Anglicans could hold office. In Scotland, the union with England in 1707 did not change the poverty of the Highlands, the slavery of the coal mines and salt pits, or the tenements of the lowland cities. The New World offered new beginnings.

After serving during the Revolutionary War, a Pennsylvania brother, Robert Patton, joined a Virginia brother, Jacob, in

Knox County, Tennessee. Robert had been captured and interned for three years. Upon exchange, he reenlisted. Jacob enlisted in Augusta County, Virginia. Did they move to that raw wilderness of Tennessee for better land or out of the insatiable wanderlust which appears to be stuck on our genes? What did they hear about the French Revolution or the new United States Constitution on the Tennessee frontier?

Jacob had nine children and Robert thirteen. Jacob's son, James Cooper Patton, enlisted in the army for the War of 1812. He was not mustered by the time the war ended. Instead, he married Robert's fourth daughter, Isabella. Did these first cousin newlyweds ever learn of the death of their countrymen at the Alamo?

The rolling hills and coves of Tennessee did not hold the James Cooper Patton family. By 1841, husband, wife and ten children had settled in Gentry County where the patriarch became a community leader and gave his name to Pattonsburg.

A bit later the Reverend Timothy Morgan walked his horse up to the Patton household. The Reverend Morgan came from Springfield, Massachusetts by way of Rochester, Vermont as a Presbyterian circuit rider. He road from community to community with his double-barreled cap and ball shotgun by his side along with his Bible. Mr. Patton was the leader of the Mt. Zion Presbyterian church. Built in 1842, it was the first church in the county. He soon agreed that Rev. Morgan would be its minister as well as his son-in-law.

The Morgan clan has Welch and Irish origins. The members have contributed to U.S. history as generals, financiers as well as at least one buccaneer. Timothy and Belinda were married in 1855 and along with the gifts came a house slave born in 1849. She cared for the five children born to the Morgans. Hearing of the Emancipation Proclamation, the Rev. Morgan told Venus she was free to go anywhere she wished. She elected to stay with the family. When Albert Morgan, the son of Timothy and Belinda, married "Lizzie" Young she went with the couple and raised their family including my maternal grandmother, Bessie Deborah.

My Grandfather Perry's origins have been traced back as far as the Carolinas and belong to the large southern Perry clan. His grandfather, James, married and had children in Macomb, Illinois. By 1856, they had all moved to Gentry County. How the civil terrorism next door in Kansas affected the farmers in Gentry County, I'll never know. This was still frontier with wolves in the dark forests and Indians nearby. Many of the Pattons were involved in forcibly moving the Fox Indians out of the region in 1847. Did they hear about the treatment of the Mormons in their own state and the great movement of the thousands of Mormons rolling across Iowa on their trek to Utah? How did these families survive without the nightly news and the daily headline? Had they heard the drums of war sounding in the south? James and Elizabeth Perry's son, Benjamin, served four years with the Union Army and carried to his grave a knot on his forehead where a musket ball had brained him. James himself was killed in a posse while chasing a horse thief.

This same Ben Perry, the first (there were three more) married Nancy Adkisson of Loderburg, Kentucky. The Adkissons traced their American origins back to William Perrin (1758-1799). William was descendent of a French Huguenot family who fled to this country after the revocation of the Edict of Nantes (1685). William fought in the siege of Yorktown (1781) before migrating to Kentucky. There he married and his daughter, Mary, married Samuel Adkisson. Samuel's son, William, arrived in Gentry County in 1856 with his wife Joanna McCoy. Nancy, their daughter and my grandfather Woodson's mother, was born in 1846.

My progenitors had converged on Miller Township of this then isolated county in northwest Missouri. Travels outside of the county were exceptional. When Rev. Morgan traveled back to the Presbyterian General Assembly in Buffalo (1853) to ask for building funds for a brick Mt. Zion Church, he wrote back briefly on the slavery debate and a much longer description of a new steel bridge to which the assembly was taken by the president of the New York and Buffalo Railroad Company. His words on the debate, which lasted more than a day, were, "The 27th of May the slavery question was up all day and not disposed of. The ultra north are [sic] inclined to carry something more decided than before. The cooler ones of the north are inclined to let it slide off easy, what will be done is not decided."

I have no idea how these people of Gentry County voted on the presidency of their Illinois neighbor Mr. Lincoln. A poignant paragraph in William Adkisson's obituary states that he always voted Republican, beginning in 1852.

I take you back to the little towns, the dirt and gravel roads, the isolated farm houses and the verdant land of pastures, hedgerows, wood lots, punctuating the fields of corn, wheat, oats, alfalfa. TIME WAS when a boy could test himself against the chores of a working farm.

Woodson and Bessie had one son who died in his first year and then my mother, Wilma Augusta. After grammar school in a one room school house to which she rode her pony, she was sent along with her cousin to "finishing school" in nearby Albany. Then she went on to the University of Nebraska in Lincoln. She met my father, Paul, at a fraternity/sorority party. They were married in 1928. The stock market crash put a lot of people out of work, but my father had a secure job as an assistant manager of a S.S. Kresge store in Chicago. I was born at Chicago Lying-in Hospital in 1932. Soon we moved to Escanaba, Michigan, then to Wausau, Wisconsin. It is there my memories of childhood begin.

Soon after my birth, Wilma took me on a bus trip for my grandparents to see their new and what would be their only grandchild. She told me that I cried all the time I was there. Local doctors could not diagnose the problem. Back at the Chicago hospital my mastoiditis was treated with surgery. In spite of this early experience, I spent my summers on the farm until it was sold in 1947.

Bessie Morgan-Perry, Lizzie Young-Morgan, Wilma Perry, Luddia Young, and Debora Jones.

1

Over the River and Through the Woods

The slush and mud of the playground at John Marshall School in Wausau, Wisconsin has turned to grass and dust. Marbles have been squirreled away like nuts in string pouches as soft ball replaces "pot" and "circle." Tennis shoes replace the lace boots with the knife pocket.

The day finally arrives! Yesterday I came running home with my notebooks, pencils and final report card. Today I stand on the lawn and watch the car being packed with suitcases, trunks and packages. There is just enough room in the back seat for a boy to curl up. Will we ever get started?

Finally, Mom says, "You ride in front until your breakfast settles." As Dad turns out of the driveway I take one last look at the neighborhood and think about the Southend Gang I am leaving for the summer. I feel an instant pang of regret as the car turns out onto the highway.

The car speeds up. The cracks in the concrete begin the rhythmic thump-thump-a-thump on the tires. I recognize less and less of the landscape: Past the paper mill with its awful smell, out through rolling farm country on two-lane roads.

Sometimes the road splits a farm house from its dairy barn and silo. Other times, long dirt roads lead to a white farmhouse surrounded by its out buildings nestled under the brow of a forest rising up to cap a hill. This is glacier country sculpted by giant hands in the form of 100 foot walls of ice.

"When are we going to get there?"

My question brings on a medley of song: "On Wisconsin" followed by "Whistle While You Work," "Oh, How I hate to Get Up in the Morning" and anything else Mom and Dad can think of.

The singing peters out with "It's a Long Way to Tipperary." Sometime later I am shifted to the rear seat as Mom begins the navigating. We stop along the roadside for some peanut butter and jelly sandwiches, along with milk and pears. The air has a steamy freshness as the sun cooks the moisture out of the hedgerows and fields.

As we cross the "Big Muddy" at Dubuque, Iowa, I strain to look over the bridge rails to see the great spread of water still brown and swirling from the spring rains. I already sense the historical significance of this great river. Something in Dad's voice as he anticipates the Mississippi crossing creates awe.

Soon a discussion about whether to stop in Cedar Rapids or Des Moines filters to the rear seat. I respond with, "When are we going to get there?"

This question causes an outburst of "We are from I-O-Way, I-O-Way, best state in the land, corn on every hand…" The words are true. Dark, plowed fields hold rank and file of green shoots, hand-high, marching to the horizon.

On U.S. 6 leading into Des Moines, Berma Shave signs break the monotony of the scenery and the thump-a-thump of the road. The highway goes directly into Des Moines. We stop next to a big, redbrick hotel.

How can Mom and Dad do this? Just a few hours from Grandad's and we're stopping for the night. Up the stairs and down a dark hall with dark carpeting. Windows at both ends allow a spooky light to filter in.

The hotel room smells closed up. One light hangs from the ceiling and another hangs on the headboard of the double bed. It's obvious that electricity has been added to the room after the building was built. The bathroom has a big washbowl, about chin high, resting on a china pedestal. The bathtub rests on claw foot legs. The water taps on the washstand read "HOT," "COLD" and "ICEWATER." The ICEWATER doesn't work.

While we eat at a local restaurant, a cot is wheeled into the hotel room. Even with the window open, its's too hot and stuffy. And I am too excited to sleep. City lights and sounds are new to this small-town boy. I lie on my back looking at the patterns on the ceiling.

My parents are all packed and ready to go to breakfast before they wake me. Once on highway 69 south of Des Moines, I am given mints to suck on to prevent car sickness. They don't work. The combination of curves, thump-a-thump and anticipation leads to my exclamation, "I'm gonna' throw up."

The auto careens to the roadside and Mom and I plunge out to the grass. Sometimes it is a false alarm, but more often the undigested pancakes or oatmeal is left along the road.

Back in the car another chorus of "We are from I-O-WAY" is followed by "There is no place like Nebraska…" Dad honks the horn as we cross the state line into Missouri. After one last chorus of the Iowa song we quiet down in anticipation of an imminent arrival.

At Bethany we turn off 69 west to Albany. South of Albany the concrete turns to gravel and I kneel behind the front seat trying to recognize some familiar landmark. Cresting the top of the hill where the gravel road turns east to McFall, Dad stops. There in the distance, on the tip of the next hill is the familiar brick farmhouse and red barn. My heart pounds madly.

The Farmhouse

Dad eases down the hill into the mud and ruts of the dirt road. Slowly grinding away he slides onto the loose planks of Crawford bridge crossing the Grand River. The boards rattle and the iron struts complain. I look straight down past the planks to the turbulent brown water below. Other times I will go swimming here and take 22 rifle practice off the bridge at moving sticks. Years later the bridge will collapse under the weight of a 18-wheeler taking a shortcut.

On the other side, Dad wallows through a huge pool of water and mud, then up a small rise past the Crawford farm. Here is where some of my summer playmates live. As the Ford grinds up the last hill, past the crossroad where the mail boxes stand on guard, Dad tries to keep the car in the ruts. But the Missouri mud will not comply this year and the car slips slowly into the ditch. Now I understand. We took time getting here hoping the roads had dried off enough for the car to get through.

I pull off my "tenneys" and socks and step into the mud. It squishes through my toes feeling slippery and cool. It is the first time I've been outside without shoes this year. As I trudge up the last 50 yards and through the front gate, there is Grandma on the front step. She smothers me with a big hug and a kiss as she exclaims, "I'll swan it's good to see you."

"Where's Grandad?"

"Hitchin' up the team."

I run around to the back screen porch and find my straw hat and overalls hanging on a hook. Cramming the straw hat on my head—it doesn't seem to fit—I rush back outside. Following the jingle of the team coming out of the barn, I hurry down the road to the car.

"Grandad, Grandad," I cry as I run slipping and sliding down a rut. Mud sucks at my ankles and splatters on my seersucker shorts. Grandad has turned the team around. I slow down to a walk as the team appears to get bigger and bigger. I still don't come up to Queen's shoulder. Grandad picks me up for a hug and a kiss. "Well, Dear Boy, you ready to work this summer?"

"Yes, I sure am, Grandad."

He plops me on Queen's back. "Now you hang on there," he warns as he goes back to hitching a logging chain onto the car. There are two horns with round brass knobs sticking out of the top of the harness. As Grandad picks up the reins, I grab each knob.

"Get up there, ho Queen, hup Jim."

The chain pulls tight, the team digs their hooves in, the motor begins to grind and the car slithers out of the ditch. The caravan of horses, driver and car turns into the barnyard and stops at the house gate. The team and I go to the barn where I climb off over Queen's shoulder onto the feed box and over into an empty stall. I'll not let her step on my bare feet.

Back at the house, with feet washed, the team let out, the car unpacked, I listen to the adults catch up on the local news. Once I learn that Grandad kept the team in the barn just in case we got stuck, and that he was sitting on the front porch waiting for us, my curiosity recedes. I study his face and the cadence of his voice until I am sure I know him again. He is tall and thin with steel-gray hair, deep-set eyes and a face that could remind you of a beardless Abe Lincoln.

Soon I get bored with the adult talk and state, "I'm gonna' look around." I need to survey what will be my domain for the next month or so.

2

Pigs, Pigs, Pigs

My domain is 160 acres with the farm house set on the eastern side along the dirt road. I leave the front living room, past the stairs to the upper three bedrooms and pass into the kitchen. There is a wood stove on the left, and several tables for food preparation and eating. Through the kitchen, the mud porch, screened with opaque wax paper, is next. Outside, directly in front of the screen door is the chicken yard. Through the gate stands a huge water oak covering the yard. It is the housing project for hundreds of sparrows who shout their good nights every evening. To the left is the two-hole, smelly, spider- and wasp-infested outhouse. To the right is the hen house with the roosts and nest boxes. Next to it stands the brooder house for the young chicks.

If I make a left turn instead of going into the chicken yard, I pass the smoke house. It's not used for smoking meat anymore but contains the washday paraphernalia. Next to it is the woodpile. I pull open the barnyard gate and head for the big, red barn on the right passing the wagon with the water tank and one of the calf pens. Past the barn is another calf pen and then the garden. The car barn where most of the tools as well as the car are kept is closer to the road, directly across from the barn yard gate. I climb up on the seat of every farm implement stationed around the barn yard: the mower, the side-delivery and sulky rakes, and the box wagon and frame for the hay wagon, a plow, a cultivator, a disk and a harrow. I guess I have begun to mark my territory.

The sun is just over the treetops on the west 40-acre alfalfa field. The first round of talk has about petered out. I have replaced my shorts with overalls which are a bit too tight this year. Grandad rises from his rocker. "Let's go feed the pigs."

I follow him to the mud porch where the "slop" buckets are kept. Grandma has been dumping the eatable garbage and day old skimmed milk in the two stainless steel buckets. Now they have a ripe odor of sour milk.

Grandad picks up one in each hand and starts out the screened door. He passes the smoke house and the pump. I open the yard gate. We go through the barnyard and into the pasture. As we start down the hill, Grandad yells in a falsetto voice, "Whooee, pig, pig, pig. Whooee, pig, pig!"

Pigs of all sizes stick up their ears and start running toward the feed lot at the bottom of the hill. Some, wallowing in the mud around the windmill, shake themselves out of the mud. "Grunt, grunt," they reply.

I try to copy Grandad's call. "Whooee pig, pig…"

The pigs running toward the feedlot stop abruptly their ears flopping forward. They turn and run saying, "Wuff, olf, oly." Others look around confused.

Grandad calls again. The pigs are reassured. They continue their ramble.

I give it another try. After a few days the pigs get used to my voice. They come, ears flapping.

At the feedlot, Grandad leans over the fence and pours the slop in a trough. The anxious pigs get the slop over their heads as they push and shove and squeal trying to stay at the trough. Grandad climbs into the lot. The opening in the fence only lets in the smaller pigs. The sows and boar are fed outside the fence. I crawl through the pig opening.

Shovels full of bright yellow ears of corn are thrown into the yard with a huge scoop. Grandad throws the first shovel over the fence to the big pigs. Then he makes a line of corn across the lot with more scoops. The pigs fight and squeal to get in the line until there is enough room for every pig. Then they spread out and settle down to rhythmic chomping and grunting. Once in a while one pig will get too close to another and a "wuff" and a sham-bite followed by a squeal ensues. The pecking order, in this case the eating order, must be maintained.

After several weeks of feeding, the lot is full of corn cobs. One morning, Grandad and I hitch up the team and pull the drag down to the lot. Grandad scrapes up the cobs into a pile, pours coal-oil on them and lights a huge bond fire.

This evening, we return to the pump at the house and rinse out the slop buckets before dropping them off at the mud porch. Then we return to the barn with a couple of stainless steal buckets. I push open the barn doors that complain with a loud screech. Slowly two or three cows amble into their respective stalls, always in the same order, always in her own stall.

Grandad has put some grain in the feed boxes and, while the cows grind and swallow, Grandad sits on a stool and milks them. The first stream of milk rings in the bucket like a muted door bell. Then, as the bucket fills, the squirt, squirt, squirt sounds like a frog croaking "Whalk, whalk, whalk."

Sometimes a bold barn cat comes meow, meowing and Grandad squirts it in the face. The cat retreats to lick the milk off. Feral cats are important in keeping down the rodent population.

When the two buckets are nearly full, Grandad calls, "Let in the calves." They have been bawling in the lot next to the barn since their moms came in. Every few minutes a mom would answer with a low mmmmmm between chews.

I open the gate and the caves charge through into the barn and slam into their mother's side. They grab a tit, bang on the udder with their heads and finish the milking. Soon the calves have taken all the milk and Grandad shoos them back into the lot. I open the barn door with the squeaky rails and the cows leave as majestically as they arrived, in the same order.

With the evening chores done, Grandad carries the milk to the mud porch. Cats with their tails in question marks follow behind him meowing. He stops to fill the cat bowls inside of the barnyard fence then empties the milk in the large flat pans in the pantry. There the cream will separate to the top and be skimmed off for cobbler or churning into butter. The pantry connects the kitchen with the dining room.

A few days into the summer, Grandad announces the "The Vet is coming today. Do you want to help catch the little pigs?"

Grandads knows I do.

When the Vet comes into the barnyard there are a few minutes of talk while waiting for Abe Burton to arrive. Abe is a neighbor who trades work with Grandad. "Well, look who's here again this summer. Perry, Abie will like to know he has someone else to play with." The men continue for a while exchanging news. Then, the Vet takes out his bag and an ice chest and we all start over to the farrowing sheds next to the garden. At the shed, the sows are grunting outside because Grandad has separated them from their piglets. A V-shaped trough is set up inside the compound. Abe says, "Okay, Perry, let's have one."

Inside of the low shed, I crawl toward a crowd of little pigs in a corner. As they spread away from me, I grab one by the hind leg. "Eeee, eeee, squeeee," it cries. The sows start wuffing and banging at the closed gate. I drag the wriggling piglet to Abe and Grandad. They hold the squirming, squealing mass on its back in the trough. The Vet shoots a flu vaccine in a leg and some worm medicine in its mouth. The squeals turn to gurgles. I go for the next piglet as Abe drops the first one in with the sows. It toddles around while the sows nudge it.

On my hands and knees in the dirt of the shed, I grab at the elusive future bacon. Dust and squeals rise out of the darkness. I back out with another squealing porker. The chain of catch, inoculate and release goes on until all the piglets are back with their moms. I'm covered with dust. My two blue eyes peer out of a grey face. The first layer is washed off down at the water tank at the wind mill. Then I take a real bath in a galvanized tub next to the pump. A kettle of boiling water heats up the chilly well water. Even though I was wearing my straw hat, the mud had to be scrubbed out of my hair. It had been a good day of honest dirt.

One evening at the feedlot, Grandad says, "I want you to catch the pigs I point out and hold them while I operate on them." Grandad takes out his pocket knife and begins sharpening it on a whet stone. The pigs are chomping peacefully on the corn. "That one." Grandad points to a black and cream one with a straight tail. I grab its hind leg. "Squee," the pig complains. I drag the protester to Grandad. He puts his knees on the pig's legs while I hold the jerking front ones. He makes an incision, cuts some flesh out, does it again and dabs some tar on the wound. The pig jumps up, shakes himself, and runs back to the line of corn. The sows outside are complaining.

I catch another one designated for the operation and begin dragging him back. Suddenly a sow crashes through the barrier. "Let him go," Grandad shouts. I stand frozen with the pig jumping and squealing in my hand and the sow rushing toward me with angry wuffs. Grandad grabs a loose two-by-four and, running toward the sow, whacks it on the head.

Stunned, the sow collapses. Grandad helps me let go of the pig, shoos the sow out and puts up a temporary barrier. "That's enough for today," he assesses. "We'll see about tomorrow."

"Grandad," I ask, "Why do you have to operate on the pigs?"

"So they grow tender meat," he answers. It is sufficient for the time being.

3

You Can't Chop Down a Whiffletree

Hanging on to a squealing pig was not the only time Grandad had to rescue me. In the barn, on the left were grain bins for oats and corn to feed the horses and cows. One day I opened one of the doors and found a large rat scampering away up a pile of grain. It couldn't get away because the rat kept slipping on the loose grain. I grabbed it by the tail and took the squeaking rodent out to show Grandad. He took one look and shouted, "Throw it away!" I just held on. He rushed over and grabbed it throwing it against the wall. Stunned, it was killed with a pitch fork.

Grandad lived long enough to learn that I handled, laboratory mice and rats, rabbits, sheep, guinea pigs, and even a monkey. I believe that my familiarity with animals on the farm made it easy for me to handle them years later.

Grandad's day begins with the rising of the chickens. Before breakfast, he opens up the hen house. The Rhode Island Reds come pouring out the door like chocolate pudding. With squawks and flutter they spread out over the chicken yard trying to find any worms that haven't taken cover. Then Grandad feeds the pigs and milks the cows. About now I climb out of the high bed with the feather mattress, pull on my overalls and stumble down stairs. At a breakfast of oatmeal and biscuits made on the wooden cookstove, Grandad slyly mentions, "Well, Pard, let's go get the team."

Sometimes the horses are at the barn waiting to be fed. Usually, they seem to anticipate when they are wanted and clump in the far back pasture. Grandad pulls the old green Studebaker out of the car barn and through the back barnyard gate. I ride on the running-board hanging on to the door then jumping off to open and close the gates.

The Team before Queen and Jim.

I am thrilled to hang on to the window as the car bumps past the pig pen and the windmill and into the meadow. I am also honored that Grandad trusts me on the precarious journey. The horses watch as the car approaches. Before the car gets close, the team skirts the edge of the meadow as the cows watch. Queen and Jim charge past the car and have arrived at the barn doors by the time I swing down to open them. I jump out of the way as the team heads for the feed bin and a measure of oats, raising dust and scattering cats. I close the doors as Grandad comes in the other side after putting the car away.

Harnessing begins.

Every year I can test my growth better than any Little Leaguer by my progress in harnessing and hitching the team. Just a few years earlier all I could do was snap the harness chest straps and walk, almost upright, under the horses to take the girth and belly band for Grandad to buckle.

This year I can lift and put on the horse collars. I'm not strong enough yet to carry and throw on the rest of the harness. It takes skill to grab the mass of leather and metal off the pegs and throw it on the horses' backs so that it is all in the right place untangled. I can push the horses' tails up over the rear breach strap. Grandad has buckled up the rest of the harness. I bring the halter for Grandad to slip over the horses' heads. Jim's halter has leather blinders so he won't see to his sides. He is a big, black gelding and enjoys shying at any provocation.

When I was younger, all I could do was hook the trace chains to the farm implement. Today I grab the reins and say, "Hup, Queen…Jim." They reluctantly leave the barnyard doorway and head toward the box wagon. Queen steps lightly across the wagon tongue. I pull lightly on the reins and shout, "Whoa, back, back, Queen back," until the team is correctly placed on each side of the tongue.

Grandad lifts up the tongue about chest high and I snap each collar to the rings of the yoke. The yoke, Grandad calls it the singletree, slips over the tongue and keeps the team lined up parallel to the tongue. It also serves as the power connection if the team must back the implement.

Next the trace chains are attached to the wagon. They have been snapped on the harness and are removed and connected to each end of a round wooden timber about three feet long. I count the number of links to hang loose before the next link is hooked: four for Queen and three for Jim. This plank, which Grandad calls the whiffletree, is attached to a doubletree, a plank about five feet long. It, in turn, is attached to the wagon tongue with an iron spike so it can pivot.

Most horse drawn wagons look about the same in all farm yards. This working wagon looked like a cheese box with wheels. The front of the box sits on an axle which pivots so that sharp turns can be made. The wagon tongue is attached to the front axle. Implements like the mower and the rakes did not pivot so the horses have to be backed up to turn sharp corners.

While I am doing my jobs circling around these draft horses, they are in constant motion. Their skin shivers as they try to shake off the invading flies. Their tails lash out nervously, sometimes swatting off my hat. Their hooves smash the dry earth with a constant beat. One stomp of these dinner plate sized hoofs could smash a boy's foot.

The whole system, team, harness, and double-, single-, and whiffle-trees have to be coordinated so that the horse power is distributed equally. Pivots and wheels are greased to lessen the friction. Once everything is in the right place, the whole system produces the song of the wagon: I climb into the wagon box with the reins and stand behind the seat. Grandad stands next to me. "Get up there," I shout in my youthful voice. I gently slap the reins, four of them, on the horses' backs. They strain forward and the wagon begins to move. I pull on Queen's reins and the team turns out of the barnyard. A rattle of loose boards and squeak of wheels begins the wagon song. Trace chains jingle like small bells. Iron-rimmed wheels bang over rocks and ruts. Jim begins grunting as if complaining to Queen about having to work on such a beautiful day. Both horses leave deposits in the road to emphasize their complaints. The smell of leather, horses, grease and dew distilling from the hedges and fields combines in a new bouquet. Larks sing their ode to the sun and red-winged blackbirds chirp their insolence. I glow with pride. I am a real farm boy going out to help Grandad fix fences.

Returning from a day's work, the team seems to be walking in slow motion until they turn into the barnyard. They move without command to the spot where the wagon belongs and stop. I let down the tongue, unsnap the traces from the whiffletrees and hook the chains on the harness, and unhook the single tree. Care is taken to fold the reins properly before they are unclipped from the bits. As soon as the halters are removed the team charges into their stall for a ration of oats. While the harness is lifted off and the collars are removed, the horses grind the oats.

White spots of dried sweat have accumulated under the leather straps and horse collars. I climb up on the stall to brush out the hair with a curry comb. Grandad slaps a gummy tar on areas of chafing. I push open the barn doors to the usual scream of rusty complaint. This is the signal for the horses to back out of the stall. Showing no sign of being tired, Queen first, then Jim charge out of the barn faster than they arrived in the morning. Halfway down the hill, Jim stops to roll in the dust trying two or three times before he goes all the way over. Queen also takes her turn but in a more dignified manner.

Now the team strolls off to add some water at the wind-mill and grass to the oats in their bellies. It is time to do the evening chores.

4

Washday Blueing

Kerbang! Bang! Pop, pop, bang!

I exploded up like a jack-in-the-box. Were the "Japs" attacking? Were the Germans shooting?

Pop, bang, bang! I slid out of the high bed and stumbled down stairs. At the first landing, I could look out on the chicken yard. Smoke covered the ground. It came from the smoke house.

Bang, pop, put, put, put. The smoke and noise were coming from a tube sticking out of the smoke house. I continued down the stars and through the kitchen to the mud porch in my bare feet and pajamas. Looking in the smoke house, I saw Grandma stirring a tub of boiling water. Grandad was putting the steaming clothes into a washing machine. The pop-bang noise came from the gasoline motor driving the washing machine.

"Well, sleepy head, it's about time you got up," Grandma shouted over the noise. "There's biscuits in the oven and fix yourself some cereal." She turned back to the boiling clothes.

I grabbed a hot biscuit on my way through the kitchen and climbed the stairs to throw on my overalls and tennis shoes. On my way back I floated some Cheerios in a bowl of farm cream. Then I sat on the back stoop and watched the washday process.

Grandad stopped the washing machine's agitation and twisted the wringer around. As he fed the properly folded clothes through the wringer, they dropped into a tub of water. The soapy water squished back into the washing machine.

"Hey, Pard, ready to go to work?" Grandads shouted.

I nodded with a mouth full of food.

"Fill up these buckets at the pump."

I set the cereal bowl on the stoop and collected the stainless steel buckets. I put one under the pump and pulled down on the handle. Metal screeched on metal. Nothing happened for a couple of handle trajectories. Then water rushed out of the faucet. I had to jump up grabbing onto the handle and ride it down, then push it up and ride it down until the bucket was full. I shoved it out of the way and put another one under the faucet. I tried to carry them in both hands like Grandad but couldn't lift them. Then I grabbed one with both hands and scrapped it along the cement path between my legs. Just then Grandad came out of the smoke house.

"That's quite a load. Here, I'll give you a hand." He took one side of the pail and we carried it to the waiting tub together. Grandma was toting a large basket of wet clothes into the chicken yard. I followed her out. She started pinning this load on the fence. An earlier load had filled most of the clothes line. Grandad's overalls, his grey socks, his grey work shirts looked as if they were marching in a row. I had forgotten about the cock-of-the-walk, the big red rooster.

Wham! Something hit me on the back and nearly knocked me down. I turned to see the rooster preparing to attack again. I recalled the battles with him. Every yearly visit he had to defend his territory from this little person whose size, early in the conflicts, nearly equaled his. In those early years the rooster had won. Then it was a draw when I remembered to carry a stick when I entered the chicken yard. Now it was time to face up to the challenger.

We stared at each other. The rooster lowered his head to charge, but I acted first. I ran past the rooster and kicked him in the tail feathers. The rooster staggered, regained his balance and turned to charge again. I pushed him in the chest with my foot and he sat on his tail. He jumped up and stalked around me trying to get behind.

I was getting braver with each success. I charged flapping my arms and yelling. The rooster turned and ran away high stepping like a band major. That was all the dignity he could muster. He scattered the hens who had been scratching in the dust with one eye on the battle. The rooster chased a few hens to show who was still boss and ignored me.

"Well, I never…," Grandma commented. "Now, look who's the head rooster." I joined her with one eye open for a sneak attack by the defeated combatant. Grandma was pinning up her print dresses. We returned to the smoke house for the "whites."

Grandad was sending the last load through the wringer. The sheets and pillowcases, white underclothes, and Grandad's white Sunday shirts soaked in the cold well water. Then he ran them into a tub of warm blue water. A cake of blueing dissolved in the water made the whites appear whiter. Finally, he ran the whites into another tub of cold water, then wrung them out. They were hung on space left on the clothes line.

The silence following the shut down of the washing machine motor was deafening. I could hear the hens clucking, the sparrows in the oak chirping, and even the buzz of the wasps in the outhouse.

Once it was clear I had established my rights to the chicken yard I could be allowed to collect the eggs in the evening. The wicker basket was kept in the smoke house. I carried it into the chicken yard and waved it at the rooster. The rooster looked, shied, and pecked the ground as if unaware of the interloper. I entered the chicken house.

Directly in front of the door was a row of twenty boxes about three feet off the concrete floor. Behind the boxes were the roosts. I went to the first box on the right and collected three eggs from the nest of straw. The next one had a red hen with her nose sticking out. I shooed her off. She squawked as she flew off and then cluck-clucked out the door complaining of the horrid treatment. I picked up two more eggs.

The hen in the next occupied nest would not shoo. I reached under her warm body and plucked out the warm eggs one-by-one. I came to one hen who would not shoo or allow me to pluck out the eggs. She pecked at my hand making me jump back frightened. The peck itself stung for a moment.

I grabbed the basket of eggs and took them to the smoke house. There was a huge egg crate that could hold twelve dozen of the brown gifts, each layer separated by a cardboard insert. I put 27 in their pockets and took six into the house.

Inside the kitchen I reported the number to Grandma and said, "We got one that's setting, Grandma." She wiped her hands on her apron and headed for the chicken house with me in her wake. She reached under the hen, taking a peck on her wrist, and grabbed the hen by her legs. The hen came squawking out of the nest hanging by her legs. "Raok, roak, roak," the hen complained, as we headed out the door to the jail. The up-side-down-hen skewed her head around trying to keep it up.

The jail was a wooden cage raised above the ground about three feet. Grandma opened a door and shoved the hen inside. She made sure there was water in the cage and closed and locked the door. The purpose of the jail was to dissuade the hens from starting a brood this time of year.

After two or three days in the jail, the hen was let out to reestablish her position in the flock. I have no evidence that jail prevented the criminal activity.

One year while playing with a hen I took her up into the barn loft and forgot her. Several weeks later I climbed into the loft again and there was the hen with about eight baby chicks. I flew to Grandad with the news. He brought the brood down. The hen clucked and fussed and headed off to the chicken yard escorted by her chicks. How she survived for the amount of time to produce the clutch without water or food I'll never know. But mother she did, ruffling up to twice her size with wings outstretched whenever her brood appeared threatened. She bossed the rooster around further diminishing his rule.

When the jail house experience was finished, we returned to the kitchen. Grandad was drinking a glass of iced tea. Soon supper was on the table. A slice of ham, store-bought white bread, fresh string beans and peach cobbler with lumpy cream.

Grandad headed for the front screened porch in his stocking feet. He rocked back in his chair with his feet on the concrete rail and looked out toward the east. On the next hill to the left was the Uncle Ben Perry's farm. Grandad pulled out a small "Between the Acts" cigar and savored the taste and smell.

I headed to the back stoop. The sparrows were making quite a fuss but there wasn't a hen in sight. They had all gone to roost. I got as far as the gate when I saw something black slithering across the chicken yard. I turned and ran to the front porch.

"Grandad, grandad. There's a black snake in the chicken yard."

Grandad turned and looked me in the eye. "You're not joshing me are you?"

"No, Grandad. Come and look…"

He slowly took his feet off the rail and headed back through the house. "You'd better not be teasing me," he warned.

"Oh, no, I'm not."

He looked over into the chicken yard and confirmed my warning. Turning back, he pulled his boots on in the mud porch and grabbed a handy hoe. Back in the chicken yard he whacked the head off the snake as it coiled and wreathed. He hung the still jerking body on the fence that had held the washed clothes just a few hours earlier.

"Black snakes are good to have around. They keep down the varmints. But they don't belong around the chickens," Grandad informed me as he stripped off his boots. "What'll we find to do tomorrow?"

5

Making Hay While the Sun Shines

This morning when I got up Grandad was gone. "He's down in the field mowing the alfalfa." Grandma answered the unasked question. "You can watch him from the back stoop."

Sure enough, I could see the team pulling the mower back and forth through the green field. I hurried back inside for the Cheerios and lumpy cream. "Don' slurp em' down, now," Grandma warned. "You've got lots of time. Grandad will be there most of the day. Now slow down."

I slurped a bit quieter. When Grandma's back was turned, I jumped up, hurried to the mud porch, stuffed on the straw hat, and headed toward the field. I climbed over the gate next to the barn rather than opening it and headed down the hill toward the pig shed. Half way down was the dry well where the small, dead animals were thrown. It was just a hole about the size of my head with a board over it so no animal would step in it. When a dead rat or some other animal was dropped, it took a long time before the thump on the bottom was heard.

I climbed through the gate to the alfalfa field and walked through the cut hay to the green patch where the mower whirred. The mower looked like a dinosaur going backward with Grandad riding on the neck and the team pulling the tail. Coming out of the body was a long arm with blades that looked like sharks' teeth. They scissored back and forth as the wheels rotated. It clattered and banged and buzzed as it sliced through the bushy plants. "Whoa-up" Grandad pulled on the reins stopping the noise machine. "Well, boy, you want to ride?"

I nodded and climbed onto the neck below Grandad's seat. I had to place my feet away from the gears which made the blades move. "Get up." Grandad gently slapped the reins on the horse's rumps which hovered over my head, tails whipping close to my straw hat. Jim grunted his usual protest as both horses stepped forward. The mower rattled and whirred, the plants fell over the blade like dominoes. The air smelled of sweet grass, hot horses and hot grease from the gear box.

When Grandad got to the end of the square, he turned right down the side, then right again, and again as the square got smaller and smaller. Suddenly, we saw a small rabbit dart out from the uncut green in front of the saw blade. "Woah," Grandad stopped the team, "Go get 'em," he shouted. I jumped off and ran after the frightened rabbit. Round and round the unmowed part of the field we ran. Finally, I dove for the little patch of brown fur and grabbed it in both hands/

"Eeee, eee, eee," cried the baby. Grandad was smiling and chuckling over the chase. I carried the shivering baby back to him.

"Well, ain't he a scrawny cuss, too little to eat." Now that I had caught him I had no idea with to do with him. "I guess we'll just have to let him go," Grandad advised. "You know you can't keep em' alive." I had captured baby rabbits before and watched them die in the cardboard box with a lot of food and water. So I took the baby over to the edge of the field and put it down. It stayed in the same spot for what seemed like a long time, then took a couple of hops and streaked for the hedge row.

We started going around the field again. After a few more rounds, the mowing monster had a fit, bucked and popped as Grandad brought it to a halt. He opened the gear box and looked inside. "Consarn it!" He walked slowly back through the new mown hay. Back and forth he walked looking down. Then he reached down and brought up a piece of iron, stuck it in his pocket and returned to the mower. Opening the tool box where I had sat, he took out a wrench and started to work. ,

"What happened, Grandad?"

"Broke an arm. Gonna' haft' fix it." The team stood stomping and swishing at flies. The morning had gotten hot and the sun was baking the juices out of the new hay. Grandad pulled out the piece of the arm and matched it to the one in his pocket. "Let's got to the blacksmith."

I unhitched the team and climbed up on Queen with some help from Grandad. We left the horses in their stall with a bit of grain. We stopped in the house to tell Grandma we were going to McFall and pulled out the Studebaker. Our dust plume followed us past Uncle Ben's, across the Grand River, past Abe Burton's farm and almost into McFall before paved road ended the dust tail. Passing Ann's gas station and the few buildings still standing including the old train depot, we drove into Johnny Hoit's yard.

Johnny came out to shake hands with Grandad, checked me out and shook hands with me too. He had huge hard hands which concealed my little mitt three or four times. "Heard you were back for the summer. Your Grandad keeping you busy?" I nodded. Johnny looked back at Grandad and they started talking about the crops, the weather, the funeral the next day, and a string of stories that stretched my patience. I wandered into the smithy.

A coke fire smoldered in the hearth. A huge anvil took center stage. Tong, hammers, pliers, bits of metal lay on tables around the hearth and anvil. I worked the bellows and sparks flew out of the coke. I picked up some metal with one of the tongs and whacked it on the anvil with one of the hammers. It jumped out of the tongs and fell to the floor. The gritty floor was made up of equal parts dirt, ashes and grease.

Johnny came in with the pieces of the rocker, pushed the coals around, stuffed the rocker in the coals and worked the billows. The coals raged turning red then white. Johnny picked out the red rocker and banged on it with a hammer. Then he put it back in the heat and repeated the banging until he stuffed it in a barrel of water. The water sizzled and steamed. Johnny held the rocker gently in his hand and looked it over. "I think this will hold up until you can order a new piece Mister Perry."

We were done. I walked out of the smithy and climbed into the hot Studebaker. I sat. Those adults weren't through jawen' yet. I got out of the car and viewed the interior of the smithy. Grandad was leaning up against a post working on a piece of wood with his knife. Johnny had his butt up against the anvil. Grandad had cut a chew and directed a stream of brown juice at the grimy floor. He worked over the area with his right boot. I wandered in and inventoried the blacksmith tools again. Then I looked at Grandad with longing eyes. I knew better than to hurry him along. I wouldn't be asked to go along with him again.

Finally, Grandad looked over, "Well, boy, you ready?" I turned and hurried to the car. This time Grandad got in. Johnny followed and leaned on Perry's door.

"You take good care of your granddad, you hear?" Johnny leaned on the window frame and started a new subject. Grandad turned off the ignition. I sat.

"Rurmmm," The Studebaker started, Johnny backed off and waved. The car turned around in the yard and headed back down the only paved street. "You wanta' share a 'Pepsi'?"

"Sure." The Studebaker turned into Ann's filling station. Ann came out as Grandad walked around the front of the car. He spit out his chaw in his hand and threw it in the bushes.

"Fill it up, Miz Miller," Grandad nodded touching the brim of his hat. Grandad always wore an old fedora rather than a straw hat. He reached into the ice cooler, pulled out a bottle and popped the cap off with the opener on the side of the chest. "Here, Pard, Have some."

"Isn't that your grandson, Perry?" Ann knew durn well who I was. "My he's gotten to be such a big boy." I took a big gulp of the soft drink. The bubbles exploded in my throat. It felt as if my throat was burning. My eyes watered. The bubbles tickled my nose. I took another swallow to wash down the burning feeling.

Ann was pumping on the gas pump with a wooden handle. The glass chamber at the top filled with orange liquid. "How's your mother and dad?"

"They're okay." Dad had driven back to Wausau alone. Mom was staying with me.

Mrs. Miller turned to Grandad as she put the hose into the car and the orange liquid emptied from a glass chamber. "That storm last Sunday gonna' help the corn any, Mister Perry?" They were on the weather and crops and next they would be on the funeral. I just hunkered down and sucked on the 'Pepsi.' Eventually, Grandad got back in the car so I followed. Ann came around to Grandad's window. He finished off the 'Pepsi' and handed it to Ann.

"That'll be a dollar-ten plus five cents for the drink." Grandad reached into the bib on his overalls and pulled out a coin purse. He put a dollar and some change in her hand.

"Much obliged," he touched his hat. The car started moving.

"You say hello to your mom for me, now, Perry." Ann waved as the car bumped onto the main road. Soon it was pulling its dust-tail back to the farm. We put the car back in the car barn.

It was time for lunch but I wasn't very hungry with the soft drink floating around in my stomach. After lunch, Grandad went back down to the field to fix the mower. I hung out on the front porch looking at the pictures in a book about famous disasters: fires, earthquakes and floods.

About four o'clock I heard the team and mower coming into the barn yard. I rushed out to help unhitch the team. The mower with its arm sticking up in the air was dropped off in its usual place. We removed the harness and let the team out.

It's time to do the chores.

6

Amuse Yourself

A few days later, I woke up to the jingle of the trace chains and the squall of the wagon wheels. I slid out of bed and stumbled to the window overlooking the barnyard. The wagon, pulling a cultivator, was just turning out of the barnyard into the road. I padded down the stairs. "Where's Grandad going?"

"He's gonna' plow the bottom land," Grandma answered, handing me a warm biscuit.

"He's not taken' me!"

"Grandad will be plowing all day and you'd get tired of that real fast. We can take him his lunch at noon."

"What'll I do all day?" I whined.

"You go get dressed and we'll find something to do. I'll call down to the Crawfords. Maybe Jo Ann can play."

"No!" I sulked. Grandad had abandoned me. "He didn't tell me he was going." My lip stuck out.

"The rooster's gonna' step on that lip. Consarn it child. He didn't want to wake you only to disappoint you. He did the chores and left. There's a lot of corn to plow…You want some Cheerios?"

"No!" I slipped off the kitchen chair and stomped up the stairs hurting my bare feet.

After I slid into my overalls and struggled with my tennis shoes, I returned to the kitchen somewhat chastised. Steam still rose from the biscuits when I cut them open and slathered strawberry preserves on the halves. I washed down the crumbly biscuits with fresh milk that had cooled from last night's milking.

"Why don't you climb the cherry tree and get enough for a cobbler?" Grandma suggested.

After downing a few more biscuits, I retrieved the egg basket from the smoke house and pulled myself up on the first limb of the cherry tree. I climbed as far as the branches would hold, as far as the second story of the house. With my eyes, I followed the road north down to the corner with the mail boxes. Turning left would take me past Temple Manering place to Bethany. Turning right would go past the Uncle Ben Perry place, the Uncle Doc Manering place and the bottom land where Grandad was plowing, past the Abe Burton farm to McFall. Going straight would take me to the Crawford farm and bridge where the pool of water stood just a few days earlier. Now a car trailed a plume of dust as it came toward the crossroad.

While I was surveying the countryside, I was stuffing ripe cherries in my mouth. Those with meat pecked out by the blue jays went into the basket. Once I was full, the basket started filling. I swung around the limbs playing pirate in the rigging like Errol Flynn. I carefully climbed down and hung onto the lowest branch with one hand while gently dropping the full basket with the other. I proudly presented the basket to Grandma.

"Well, I'll swan. That'll make a fine cobbler. You seed em' while I stir up the dough." She threw some dry corn cobs and some kindling in the wood stove. The coals were still warm from breakfast and it wouldn't take much to get the oven hot enough for baking.

"What'll I do now, Grandma?" I whined when the cobbler was in the oven.

"Well, boy, you jus go en' find something. I've got mending to do."

I let the screen door on the mud porch slam as I jammed on my straw hat. For the next hour I wandered over my domain. I visited the farrowing shed and climbed onto the corrugated iron roof. It was beginning to get hot. From there I could look south to the Hovey Manering and Chever Manering farms separated by the dirt road that ran past our farm. The hired hand there had a boy and two girls I could play with sometimes. The older boy, J.C., taught us to play doctor.

I climbed the ladder into the hay loft. The heated air vibrated with the sweet odor of hay. The barn swallows flew in and out of their mud nests. I climbed the mound of hay and slid down. I looked down the feeder holes where the hay was thrown to the stock. I chased the long-legged calves with their runny behinds in their lot trying to catch one by the tail. I shot my BB rifle at the sparrows in the oak tree in the chicken yard. Never did hit one. I climbed on top of the red, rusty water tank that Grandad used when the farm well ran dry. I shouted down the hole on top to hear my voice echo inside.

I shoved some ears of corn in the sheller and cranked out the grain into a bucket. The cob popped out the other end. I took the grain to the chicken yard and tossed it. "Chick, chick, chick!" The hens came clucking, but the rooster kept his distance.

Grandma called, "It's time to take Grandad his lunch."

We got in the old Studebaker and made dust toward the Grand River. Grandad's bottom land was just before the other bridge across the river. It seemed that every year Grandad put in a crop, the river flooded dumping more soil on the bottom and Grandad replanted. The corn would be late again this year. There he was on the cultivator riding though knee high corn. He waved, finished the row, unhooked the team and drove them to a water trough behind the Manering place. After watering them he drove them into the shade near the wagon. He put out some oats for them and headed toward the car.

While the team ate, Grandad opened his lunch bucket and chewed on a ham sandwich. "Well, Pard, what you been doen' this morning?" He swigged on some ice tea.

"Nothen," I replied. "When you comen' home?"

"When I finish. I'll be home in time to listen to the Lone Ranger." Grandad lay back under the oaks and closed his eyes. It was time for a nap. The cicadas sawed their song and the team swished their tails and shook the harness at the flies. I returned with Grandma.

It was hot. I sat out on the front screened porch reading *Black Beauty* for the twenty dozenith time. I paged through the pictures in *The Dark Continent*, a book about Africa and slavery.

I went into the guest bed room and cranked up the Victrola. Mom had quite a collection of records before she married. I listened to Harry Lauder singing about the "Good Ship Kangaroo." Then I played songs from the first World War: "Frenchy" and "Over There." There was a precursor of Amos and Andy called "The Two Black Crows." There were Victor Red Seal records of opera arias and classical music. I could slow the speed so that the voices sounded real loooow.

Some days, when Grandad was gone, Grandma did call the Crawfords. The crank phone was in the dinning room hanging on the south wall. Two shorts and a long, the bells rang on the front. It was a party line and anyone could pick up and listen to conversations. Gossip traveled fast. The operator could listen into all the conversations. She frequently knew where people had gone when they didn't answer the ring. "Hello, Bessie, the Crawford women went into town and the men are out."

I didn't want to play with Jo Ann anyway. I'd have to walk down to her house. "What you want to do?" "I don't know. What you want to do?" "What shall we do?" After wandering around their outbuildings for a while we'd end up playing house. I could have done that at home with the Hammerla girls across the street. I didn't come to Missouri to play house. I was becoming a man.

After the Second World War, Grandad bought a mare, Jenny, for me to ride. It was an extravagance since I was on the farm only a relatively short time. I guess Grandad rode her a lot during the seasons when the roads were bad. But I did ride her when we got the horses in the barn. Once she was accepted by the team she ran with them usually in the back pasture when we wanted her. I was able to saddle her and set out on my exploration of the countryside. At times I went to the woods where Grandad kept some unimproved land. It was dark and scary. I was sure there were still wolves and Indians lurking in the shadows. Sometimes I stopped at Uncle Ben's farm. Aunt Florence was just as loving as Grandma. She was a Patton and one of the first in the world to use insulin when it was new.

One day I rode down past the Hovey Manering farm. Clattering across the bridge up to the church, Jenny took it on herself to shy sideways. I slipped to the right and the tongue of the saddle gert dug a hole in my knee. Leaking blood, I headed into the Manering place. Mrs. Manering put a bandage on the wound and called Grandma on the crank telephone. I rode Jenny back up the hill and was taken into Albany to the doctor. He sewed me up and put an aluminum splint on to keep me from ripping out the stitches. Of course I did in the next few days and still have the scar to prove it.

But today, back at Grandad's I made a tent with two rocking chairs turned over and covered with a blanket. I made believe I was in the army. That didn't last long either.

I sat in one of the swings on the front porch and watched the road for the team. It was quiet except for the cicadas. Finally, they came over the hill in front of Uncle Ben's. I ran to the mud porch for my hat and headed down the road to meet them.

I met them at the cross roads and climbed in the wagon. We rattled, banged, squeaked and grunted up the hill where Dad had been stuck. We unhitched the team and let them out. Then we went into the living room to listen to, "From out of the past come the thundering hoof beats of the great horse Silver. The Lone Ranger rides again." This was the only radio program Grandad listened to other than the stock market reports. It was a weekly ritual. We could not do the chores until the Lone Ranger was over.

7

More Hay

The weather remained hot and dry after the alfalfa was cut. Grandad went down to the field every day to check the state of desiccation. One morning he decided it was time to rake the hay. We hitched up the team to the side-delivery rake and headed down to the field.

I rode on the tongue between Queen and Jim at Grandad's feet. When Grandad engaged the mechanism, long rods began to spin kicking the hay into a row. It was another noisy job as the tongs banged and the wheels clattered. The team traversed the field leaving a long row of hay pilled in its wake. I got bored and jumped off at the end of a pass through the field. From the top of the hill the field was beginning to look like an ocean with long ripples headed toward the shore.

Grandad kept his ear to the radio to determine if it was going to rain. If it did, he would have to turn the hay with the side-delivery rake and wait for it to dry again. Plans were made to put the hay in the barn the next day. We hooked up the sulky rake and headed toward the field again. Now Grandad drove over the rows. He let the rake blades fall on a row of hay. Bang! A bunch of the dried alfalfa rolled up within the jaws. When he pushed on a foot lever, the blades rose with the turn of the wheels. Rattle, bang, thump! The tines came back down to grab another bite of hay. He was making bunches of hay. Instead of rows the field was dotted with mounds of hay. It looked like drop cookies on a cookie sheet.

The next morning the team was already hitched to the hay wagon when I got up. The men were gathering in the barn yard. Abe Burton was there with a boy a few years older than I called Frank. I joined the crew after another hurried breakfast. We rode the hay wagon down to the field and started between the mounds of hay. Two men walked along side the wagon pitching the balls of hay into it with four-pronged, long-handled pitch forks. One man stacked the hay in the wagon and kept the team moving slowly down the field.

The hay gradually built up in the wagon. It was waist high, then shoulder high. The horses walked slowly enough so the men could walk up to a mound, stick a fork in it, lift it up on a shoulder, toss it onto the wagon, then turn and walk to the next mound. Soon the men were tossing it up to the stacker who would take it off the fork. Grandad decided it was a load and we headed toward the barn. We went into the barn yard and stopped under the overhang of the barn roof.

The barn loft had a great gaping mouth where the swallows flew into their nests. Coming out of the window was a long rope reaching to the ground. Pulling on this rope brought a great pair of iron jaws out to the edge of the overhang. Abe yanked on the trip rope and the jaws came crashing down on the hay. Abe placed the jaws over the hay. Now it was time for the "rick horse" to go to work.

Queen was unhitched and driven to the field side of the barn. Here she was attached to a whiffletree on the end of a rope which ran through wheels all the way to the jaws. Frank started Queen pulling toward the pig shed. On the other side, a ball of hay shook itself as it rose up to the loft and hooked onto a rail which ran into the barn. Grandad watched the ball of hay work its way across the loft. "Woah," he shouted above the scream of the metal on metal. "Woah," repeated Abe as he pulled on the trip rope. The hay plunged to the floor.

Frank unhooked the whiffletree. Abe pulled the monster back on the protesting track until it hit the end. Then it dropped like an eagle after a fish pulling the whiffletree with it. The whiffletree raced back to the barn like a frightened pig.

Now I understood why you have to unhook the whiffletree. It would hurt Queen otherwise. Frank reconnected the trace chains and the process started all over again. After a few more times I searched out Grandad. "Grandad, let me try now. I know how." Grandad talked to Frank and they both watched as I led Queen back to the whiffletree and attached the trace chains.

"Okay, let her go," Grandad yelled. I pulled on Queen's lead rope. Her ears worked back and forth for a second, then she seemed to smile, put her head down and lunged forward. I heard the mechanical mouth slap into the runner and squeal along the track.

"Woah! Hold it, woah!" Everyone was making sure I would stop. I did and unfastened the chains. The whiffletree snuck back to the spot where all the ground had been scraped by its frantic trip to the barn, gave a leap and hurried back. I started the process all over again. Grandad went back to the loft. Frank watched for a while. Then Abe yelled, "Bring Queen around."

We had emptied the first load of hay. I helped hitch Queen up to the wagon, then rode back to the field. There wasn't much that I could do loading the hay. I would only get in the way of the routine. When we headed back to the barn, I opened and closed the gates and hung on to the rear boards of the wagon going up the hill. I unhooked Queen and led her back to the well-worn path behind the barn. No one was going to take my job. Frank watched the hippopotamus jaws drop into the hay. Then he helped in the loft.

Every so often, Grandad would throw salt over the growing mound of hay. Apparently, it was a way of preventing spontaneous combustion. Grandad had lost a barn due to fire. I don't recall whether it was lightening or spontaneous combustion.

Queen and I got into a rhythm of where we had time for me to rub her nose or legs and she would wink and shake her ears knowingly. Soon another load was in the barn. I lost track of the number of loads but soon enough it was time to eat. The horses were watered and fed. We went to the mud porch to wash up. With their hats off the men all had a band of white on their foreheads where the sun hadn't reached their faces. Grandma and another woman had been cooking all morning.

In the dinning room, the men sat in their stocking feet piling on the food as it came around: Stewed apples, fried chicken and pork chops, biscuits, white bread, whipped potatoes, noodles, iced tea, green beans, peas, corn, farm butter, fresh peaches with lumpy farm cream, cakes and pies and cobbler. And talk. Talk I don't understand about hog prices and crops. But I do hear Grandad praise me. "Wasn't that some kind of boy to do all that this morning? You don't have to do it this afternoon. We have Frank to do it."

My stomach took a terrible turn so I thought I was going to throw up. "But, I want to Grandad." I think I whined.

"Okay, Pard, as long as you can keep up at it."

The men, in their stocking feet, moved out to the rocking chairs on the front porch or out to the shade of the oak trees in front. They talked quietly or napped during the heat of the day. Cicadas and sparrows and the women eating and cleaning up are the only voices. After this pause to digest the huge farm dinner the men stuff their feet back into their boots, pick up the team and wagon, and trek back to the field.

I am in charge of the water jug. It is stuck in the shade of the hedge row. It is a small wooden barrel with a wooden plug. Again and yet again the wagon is stripped of its load until the field is cleaned of the piles of hay.

Back at the barn, with the last iron mouthful of hay dumped in the loft and the horses unharnessed and chomping on their oats, the men stand in the barn yard around Abe's truck. Grandad pulls out his coin purse and pays Frank. Then, in front of the men, Grandad hands me some money. "Here, Pard, you worked Frank's job today, you get his wage." I feel something important has happened. I have become more a man this day. The men smile, get in the truck and wave as they leave Grandad and me standing together. It's time to feed the pigs and milk the cows.

I could hardly stay awake long enough for a cold piece of chicken with milk and biscuits.

But the haying season wasn't over yet. The cut alfalfa would produce a second crop. In the mean time Grandad had corn to plow and the garden to weed. Some days I would sit on the front porch and watch the heat rise off the Manering corn field across the road.

One afternoon the sky turned dark. The birds and cicadas turned silent. Off in the west big dark clouds with white edges were moving fast. Everything took on a greenish hue. Grandad came out to the porch and said, "We're in for a storm." Not a leaf twitched on the oak trees. "You get ready to go to the storm cellar."

The storm cellar was on the north side of the house near the cherry tree. It was dug into the ground about eight feet and covered with a mound of earth looking a lot like the one in the "Wizard of Oz." It had a door over the stone steps leading down to a second door to the cellar itself. The steps and the cellar were full of spider webs. It smelled of musty wet earth. Along the sides were shelves with jars of home made preserves and vegetables.

The wind came up pushing the dust down the road in great clouds. The chickens had long gone to shelter in the chicken house complaining as they piled through the open door. Grandma closed the door so it wouldn't bang. The oak branches began to whip back and forth sending sparrow nests kiting into the farm house yard. Off to the west a cloud stuck a tentative finger toward the ground. "That's a twister," Grandad said in a higher than normal voice. "We'd better get on down."

Grandad lit the white gas lantern and everyone except Grandad entered the shelter. He stood on the top step and watched the clouds and wind. Soon the rain came and with it hail; we could hear it rattling on the outside door and banging on the vent pipe. I sat on a camp stool and surveyed the glass jars sprinkled with dust. I could tell which were the tomatoes and beans but some of the other jars were a mystery.

The wind groaned and moaned around the pipe. The lantern hissed. Then it was quiet. Grandad peeked outside. Rain was still splattering on the house, but the green color was gone. Bright patches of blue sky followed after the clouds. I passed Grandad to view the damage. Little had changed except the bunches of oak leaves on the ground. The air smelled fresh like clothes right off the line.

"Perry, go let the hens out," called Grandma. When I opened the hen house door, the chickens came charging out like a football team out of a tunnel. They wanted the first opportunity to find the worms and bugs brought out by the storm. They scattered over the yard and fields scratching, pecking and clucking their good fortune.

Grandad looked down at the alfalfa field. "We'll have to put off mowing the alfalfa another day. The plants are too wet. Maybe we can hay next Friday if it doesn't rain by Thursday."

Perry and Grandfather.

Friday we hayed. During the week Grandad had cut the hay, raked it as usual and put it in the piles for collection. However, this time we would build a stack in the middle of the hay field. Harvey Manering with his team was added to Abe and his tractor to make up the crew. The Manering horses had a fork rake in front of them so they pushed it along the ground. As they traveled down a row of mounds, the hay collected in the rear of the rake. Abe had somewhat the same contraption in front of his tractor, but it had a power takeoff so the load could be lifted and dumped. The rakes brought the hay to the stack.

Soon they were putting their loads in the teeth of another contraption. When I led Queen on a rope away from this monster, it flipped the load over onto the stack. It worked somewhat like a catapult in slow motion.

The hay piled up as the forks scoured the field. I lead Queen and the stack grew. We got one stack built before dinner. After the usual farm meal and rest, we began the routine again, Another stack, another path worn by Queen and me out from the catapult. Queen began to snort her boredom and walked with more deliberation. I was tired too. But I was not going to quit. We were almost done.

Grandad stopped to do the pig chores. We kept on piling on. Abe turned off the tractor and began to cover the stacks with tar paper. The tar paper was held down with wire connected on both ends to fence posts hanging on each side of the stack. I unhooked Queen and fastened the trace chains to the harness. Then I climbed up behind her collar and gently poked her in her ribs. She snorted and headed toward the barn. The Manering team was ahead of us. Grandad had returned and rode with Abe on the tractor.

At the barn I slid off Queen and pushed open the barn door. It screeched its usual complaint. Queen ambled into her stall and stamped her feet until I dumped some oats into her feed bin. The men were standing in the barn yard jawin' again. Harvey Manering climbed on his rake and headed his team out onto the road. Abe waved and started the tractor. He yelled something which was drowned out by the motor. He pointed to the hay field.

I turned to see it soft in the evening light. It looked as if two loaves of bread had risen out of the field. Grandad put his arm on my shoulder, "Another good job, Pard. Let's have supper. Tomorrow we'll go to Albany for the band concert."

As tired as I was my heart jumped when I was reminded of the Saturday band concerts. It was my favorite time in Albany. Well, almost my favorite. Listening to the men talk was my favorite.

8

Saturday Night Band Concert

Saturdays started as any other day. Grandad was up with the sun doing the chores. Then he ate breakfast. Following breakfast, he shaved in the kitchen with hot water out of the reservoir on the cook stove. First, he stropped the razor strap with the straight razor. He slapped it back and forth several times. Then he lathered up his face with his shaving brush and soap. I could hear the blade scratching the whiskers off something like the sound of sandpaper on wood. His face became shinney pink as the lather came off and was flipped into the hot water.

Morning was filled with small jobs that had been put off during the week: repairs to wooden fences, mowing the yard. Maybe he would hitch up the team and drag the road reducing the size of the ruts. The day would go slowly for me. I was just a tag-a-long waiting for the trip to Albany.

One year, at sundown, we drove into a pasture near McFall. There was a big sheet hanging in the middle of the pasture. Chairs and benches faced the sheet. We had to watch our step to avoid any fresh cow-pies. As soon as it was dark enough, moving pictures appeared on the temporary screen. I recall the movie was a Tarzan with Cheetah, Boy and huge spiders as big as dinner plates. It was pretty scary for a boy who had left in the middle of Snow White. On another vacation we drove to a real movie theater and saw *The Northwest Mounted Police*. But Albany was our goal today.

Around dinner time we came in to eat and change our clothes. Grandad and I had fed the pigs early. We had cold chicken, corn, potatoes and stewed apples with cream. I wore Levis rather than the overalls. Grandad had on his new overalls and grey shirt. We headed for the car barn and brought the car around for Grandma. "Wellll, I'll swan, you're raren' to go to Albany?" I nodded. Gandad drove through the barnyard gate and began to make a plume of dust as he passed the house.

Down to the crossroads with the mail boxes, past Grandad's wheat field where I worked with the thrashers one August. Past the Crawford farm, over the Crawford bridge with its loose boards. At the top of the hill, we hit the gravel road and turned left to Albany. Past the turn toward Gentryville the road became concrete with the thump-thump of the tires on the cracks. We passed the mill on the edge of town where Grandad took his corn to be ground into chicken feed. The interior of the mill was always covered with a white film of flower. Then Albany.

Grandad found a diagonal parking place near the bank which was situated on the south side of the court house square. The court house was built of red brick with towers and surrounded by huge elm trees. We piled out, Grandma to start shopping and Grandad and I to the bank. "Hello, Mister Perry!" said the teller. "My that must be your grandson. He's getten' farmhand size."

"Oh, he's a worker all right." Grandad answered as he signed some papers and took away some money.

The first stop was at a local bar on the west side of the square. Grandad sat on a stool at the bar and I climbed up on another. As the bartender drew a glass of beer for Grandad, the men along the bar said howdy and started talking about things I didn't understand. While I sucked on a straw stuck in a coke of some kind, they talked while Grandad slowly sipped his beer. I was finished long before he swung off the stool and started out the door with several pauses for last words.

Out on the sidewalk, "'Low Woodson, 'low Mister Perry,'" came from the crowd of people surrounding the court house.

Woodson Perry, Wilma, Bessie, and friend in 1910.

In front of the stores, benches held elderly men sitting and staring at the courthouse as they made their desultory talk about the same things they had talked about for years. Grandad would stop and talk with some of them. They would always have to comment on his grandson. "That Wilma's boy?" "He's a fine looking worker there."

Turning the corner to the north side of the square, I could see the men hanging around the pump near the court house building. A tin cup hung on the rod that went up and down when the pump-handle was pumped. It was the community cup for all to use.

We wandered into the hardware store. Grandad wasn't looking for anything special, just touching and examining. "Can I hep you Mister Perry," a man in a blue apron asked.

"No thanks, jus looken," he replied.

The afternoon turned into evening. Lights came on around the square. I didn't say a word, but Grandad looked at me and said, "You be back at the car right after the concert.

"Yes, sir,"

I headed for the bandstand at the northwest corner of the court house lawn. Uniformed men were arranging their seats and music stands. The squeaks, howls and bangs of the instruments brought out the children to ogle.

"What's your name?" A girl slightly taller than I asked. She was wearing a white dress with pink ribbons.

"Perry."

"Oh you're Uncle Woodson and Aunt Bessy's grandson. I'm Amy. Let's play tag. You're it." She pushed me and ran. I followed her around the courthouse, but couldn't catch her. There were other children nearby so I touched one of them and cried, "You're it."

I turned back to the bandstand. The band had begun to go "Umpa, umpa," together. Years later I would recognize the standard Sousa marches.

Around the bandstand, the gang of children ran seemingly as fast as the music. The lightening bugs were out and we chased them. I skidded in the dew moistened grass. Of course there would be grass stains to get out on washday. Faces got red and bodies smelled of sweet prepubescent sweat. Boys wrestled and girls giggled and ran hand-in-hand together.

The band had stopped. "I gotta' go," I said to no one in particular.

"Bye, see you next time," followed me around the bandstand.

I got back to the car about the same time as everyone else. "You have a good time?" Grandma asked.

"Ya."

"You meet any children?"

"Ya, Amy,"

"Amy who?"

"Don't know. She had on a white dress."

We drove up to the grocery store. There waiting for us were several paper sacks to be put in the trunk of the car. That job done we drove a few blocks north to the frozen food locker to pick up the week's supply of meat. It was the meat Grandad had butchered in the fall and winter. Then we headed home.

The headlights cut a hole in the darkness. Some lights still glowed in nearby farm houses. The car lights reflected off the eyes of cats hunting along the road. Sometimes green eyes sparkled along the fence line where the darker shapes of horses or cattle stood. I was so tired I couldn't keep my eyes open. This dark world was unfamiliar like traveling through a tunnel. The car bumped from concrete to gravel.

I awoke when we clattered across Crawford bridge. Soon were we at the yard gate. When I opened it, it made its usual screeching complaint. I swung the pump handle up and down. The pump also banged and complained until the water gushed out. I stuck our tin cup underneath before the stream stopped. The cold water tasted metallic and refreshing.

Grandad made several trips with the groceries. Then he put on his work overalls, lit the lantern and headed for the barn. The calves were bawling about their situation. The cows were comforting them with low mooooos. They stuck their noses through the wire fence. Grandad slid open the barn doors and the cows tumbled into their respective stalls. He took about a pail of milk then let the caves in for a good meal.

Before the calves had finished, I was in bed and asleep.

9

Sunday Go to Meeting

Grandad still had to feed the stock on Sundays. Grandma put laying mash in the troughs for the chickens and filled their water jugs as usual.

Grandad milked the cows. The horses were in the back pasture. They looked up when they heard the scream of the rusty track when the barn doors opened. When they didn't see the Studebaker head their way they went back to their lazy grazing.

After a breakfast of oatmeal and biscuits, he went through his shaving routine. Then he went up the stairs to shake me out of my dreams. "Ho, boy, time to get dressed for church. Grandma's got breakfast ready." I pulled on my shorts and white shirt and stuffed my feet into the sneakers. Grandma had a boiled egg and toast waiting when I came back from the outhouse.

She had an apron on over her flowered, print dress. A large picnic basket was being layered with food. When I peered in, Grandma answered my unasked question, "Church picnic today."

Grandad, in his dark suit, white shirt and dark tie had brought the car to the yard gate. He helped Grandma with the food basket. We headed off toward McFall although there was a church not a mile away south past the Manering farms. We were headed for the McFall Methodist Church that Grandma had joined as a young woman. It was white with a belfry and many steps going up to the front doors. Cars had collected haphazardly around the church.

Grandma took me to the cellar door and down the stairs into a dank basement. There were some kids sitting in little chairs. "Good morning, Bessie. Who's this young fellow? That's not Wilma's boy?" While they traded complements, I smelled the damp mildew of the basement which had been closed all week

"Well you jus' sit down with the rest of the children. My how you've grown since last summer."

While Clara talked about the Bible and Jesus, the children snuck peaks or just ogled me and wormed and squirmed. Later we all put a penny in a box labeled "Missions." Clara herded us up the stone stairs and then into the church like a sheep dog. We were ushered into one of the front pews, the boys elbowing each other and harassing the girls

Grandad and Grandma were sitting in the choir loft next to the lectern. Soon the service started. I could hear

Grandad's high-pitched voice pleading, "Come, come, come, come to the church in the wildwood…"

The minister preached, the choir sang, someone who had a birthday dropped some money in another jar labeled Missions, more singing, some announcements and finally the last hymn. I waited for Grandad to come down from the choir loft. As we left, there were what had become the usual comments about "Wilma's boy." I was getting the feeling that Wilma was some kind of a famous person in Gentry County. To me she was just Mom.

The parishioners were standing around below the steps talking up a storm. Talk, talk, talk.

They were doing their "yard work." Catching up on the week's gossip. Sometimes invitations were made to "drop by" or, more formally, to "come have dinner with us."

On those visits there was nothing for me to do except explore new farm yards. They were all about the same even thought laid out differently. There always was a hen house. Some contained white Leghorns, others grey Guineas that cackled rather than clucked. There would be a garden, fruit trees, out buildings of various shapes, farm equipment to climb on and sometimes a grinding wheel to turn.

One Sunday we visited the old Morgan home place where Grandma was born. I walked in to find an old black woman snapping beans at the kitchen table. The kitchen was hot with two stoves running to cook Sunday dinner for a batch of relatives. The black woman looked up, squinted at me and smiled. She only had two or three teeth left. "I'll bet this is Wilma's boy," she croaked. "Come here boy and let Venus see you."

Venus Morgan (by the tree) and the Morgan Family.

I was placed on her lap. She was so old and dark she made me nervous. I sat there as long as I could, then slipped down and out the door. This was my first and last meeting with a former slave. I was not familiar with black people at the time. The only ones I ever saw were porters on the trains.

Grandma told me about her some time after her death the day before Pearl Harbor. She was six years old when she was given to my grandmother's mother on her wedding day by her father in 1855. When my grandmother's father learned of the Emancipation Proclamation in 1863, he told Venus she was free to go. She disappeared and, when discovered crying in the smoke house, she said, "You don't want me any more."

Albert Morgan said she could stay as long as she wanted so she stayed with the Morgan family until her death nearly 80 years later. She raised my grandmother and her siblings. When my mother went to "finishing school" in Albany with her cousin, Aunt Venus went with them, more as a duenna than a maid for two fifteen-year-old girls in 1917.

But this Sunday was a church picnic. Everyone caravanned to a park with a stream and some swings, a teeter-totter, a slide and jungle-gym. While the children tried out all the equipment and established a pecking order, food was deposited on large folding tables and card tables. By the time the tables were full and dinner was announced someone had fallen in the creek, someone had been scraped, cut or bumped and had to run screaming to parents. Once a girl broke her arm and once a boy split the palm of his hand on the monkey bars.

A plate piled high with food could make everything better: buttered noodles, several varieties of fried chicken, potatoes whipped or boiled with more butter or a white chicken gravy, cold meats, beef, ham, cucumber salad, fruit salads, fruit and marshmallow salads and deserts. Oh, the chocolate cakes, angel-food cakes, apple-, cherry- and peach-cobblers, cookies, and several colors of jello shaking like belly dancers. It was like being back at my father's candy counter. So much. When I returned to our blanket spread out on the grass, Grandma commented, "I do believe that the boy's eyes are bigger than his stomach.

Now the talk-talk was reduced to desultory mumblings between bites. What was left at the tables on the first round soon disappeared with second helpings by those who might have missed something the first time. Soon the women collected in clumps to talk women-talk and the men stretched out on the blankets for a quick nap. Of course every woman had to be complimented on her offering and asked for her recipe. The cicadas buzzed and the children slowly clotted together for quieter games.

Half way through the afternoon someone yelled, "Are you ready to go swimming?"

The children came running with "yeses." The picnic divided into the cleaner-uppers and the swimmers. While the food was packed away in some of the cars, others took the swimmers to a real cement pool several miles away.

Sometimes the picnic ended up in the muddy waters of the Grand River, but this time we would refresh in blue, chlorinated water.

At the pool Grandad warned me, "You go in and put your trunks on but don't go in the pool until someone else is in there." I hurried into the bathroom to shuck off my clothes. I was the first one out of the dressing room. There was clear, blue water so inviting for a hot, sticky boy. I would just jump in the shallow end. I was a Boy Scout wasn't I.

Off the side of the pool I went. Down feet first for the bottom. But the bottom wasn't there. The water closed over my head. I heard roaring in my ears. My eyes searched for the surface. I clutched at the water trying to climb up. If only I could reach the side of the pool there was a net I could climb.

I broke the surface and grabbed a bit of air and a lot of water. I started down again. The roaring in my head was louder.

Grandad stood clutching the chain-link fence between him and the pool. "Grab that boy," he shouted at a stranger. "He's drowning." The man leaned over and caught my hair the next time I came up. He pulled me to the net and I climbed out. We walked over to Grandad.

"You come on out, now," were his only words to me.

As I walked back to the dressing room, I heard him say to the man, "If I hadn't walked around the building and seen him jump in I think he would have drowned."

When I joined Grandad on the other side of the fence, all he said was, "You go over en' sit on that picnic table en' wait for the rest of the children to have their swim. You didn't listen to me."

I was glad to be by myself for awhile. I knew Grandad was mad at me. Maybe he wouldn't be so mad by the time to do the chores.

10

Lambing Season

In the spring of 1940, my parents decided to take a trip to Florida. They made arrangements with my third grade teacher that I was to complete a plan of study by the time they returned. Instead of going to Florida, I was dropped off at the farm. They went on without me.

Every day I had reading to do. My grandmother had been a school teacher, in the same one room school house where Mom had ridden her pony to school, before Bessie married Grandad. Then some math problems to do. Then a letter to write to tell the students back home what I was doing on the farm. I had to read them to the class upon my return.

It was cold! It was really cold climbing out of the warm, down covers in the morning. I grabbed my clothes and hurried down stairs to dress in front of the cook stove. It was always warm in the kitchen by the time I woke up.

Grandad was the first to get out of bed. He threw some dry corn cobs in the stove, piled some kindling on top, doused it with coal-oil and lit it. Soon the stove was roaring and larger pieces of wood could be thrown in.

I actually was allowed to make the kindling out of the logs chopping the pieces thinner and thinner with a hatchet. My other major job was keeping the wood box full as well as supplying the corn cobs and kindling.

Sometimes we lit a fire in the living room fire place. There was no central heat. Electricity had come to the farm a short time before. Grandma did get an electric stove and a cream separator. The cream separator was never used and resided in the dank basement.

Before electricity they used kerosine lamps for light. Grandad still used the lanterns for the barn. He never had electricity put in the out buildings. There was a large yard light at the barnyard gate. Before electricity, Grandad had tried acetylene for light. There was a cistern underneath the dinning room window that still smelled of acetylene. And there were gas fixtures spotted around the house. I don't remember much before electricity.

I do remember a ritual which had to be performed every year. Sometime early on during the visit I would plead for Grandad to sing the Gentleman Frog song. I am sure that is the first contact I had with him. It had Appalachian origins stretching back to the British Isles. He would set me on his knee when I was younger and sing:

Gentleman frog a-courtin' he did ride, uh-huh.
Gentleman frog a-courtin' he did ride,
A sword an' pistol by his side, uh-huh, uh-huh.
He rode up to Miss Mousie's door, uh-huh.
He rode up to Miss Mousie's door,
Where he'd often been before, uh-huh, uh-huh.

He took Miss Mousie on his knee, uh-huh.
He took Miss Mousie on his knee,
Said Miss Mousie will you marry me, uh-huh, uh-huh?

Oh no I can't do that, uh-huh
Oh no I can't do that,
Till I ask my Uncle Rat, uh-huh, uh-huh.

Uncle Rat came trippin' home, uh-huh.
Uncle Rat came trippin' home
Who's been here since I been gone, uh-huh, uh-huh?

A very wary Gentleman, uh-huh.
A very wary Gentleman,
Says he'll marry me if he can, uh-huh, uh-huh.

Where shall the weddin' supper be, uh-huh?
Where shall the wedding' supper be?
Way down yonder in a hallow tree, uh-huh, uh-huh.

First there came was a broken-back flea, uh-huh.
First there came was a broken-back flea
Followed then by a bumble bee, un-huh, un-huh.

Uncle Rat he tied the knot, uh-huh.
Uncle Rat he tied the knot
A picayune was all he got, uh-huh, uh-huh.

Gentleman Frog he jumped in the lake, uh-huh.
Gentleman Frog he jumped in the lake
An' there he was swallowed by a big black snake, uh-huh.

The big black snake he swam to land, uh-huh.
The big black snake he swam to land
There he was killed by a little, old man, uh-huh, uh-huh.

The little, old man he went to France, uh-huh.
The little, old man he went to France
An' that's the end of my romance, uh-huh!

Grandad enjoyed singing that and one about old Tom Tucker singing for his supper. Years later I looked up the "Froggie Went A-courten'" song and found about six variations to the lyrics. None were quite like Grandad's.

One evening Abe Burton came by and we all went down to the pig shed. One side had been turned into a sheep shed and ewes were birthing their kids. Some were having trouble. Abe reached into one and struggled to pull the lamb out.

One ewe was too weak to take care of her new baby. Abe took the lamb and rubbed it all over with one that had just been born. The mother checked out her new twins and decided the added lamb was hers.

Shaky legged lambs sucked on their mothers, baaaed and bumped into each other.

I had a lot to write about the next morning.

The next year Grandad did not raise sheep. When I asked him why, said that they got a liver disease in the south pasture. The Manerings, just farther south, always kept sheep so I concluded that Grandad just didn't want the bother.

With the coming of electricity came other improvements. One year there was a mail box at the road in front of the house instead of at the cross roads. I don't recall whether that was before or after the road was graveled past the house. My last visit was in 1947. By that time Grandad had a small tractor. He still used the team but most plowing, disking, and harrowing was done with the tractor. He didn't let me drive it although at 13 I was old enough.

11

The Last Day

My last day on the farm started like every other. The sun was up before I was. Grandad was sitting in the front room reading the paper for the hog prices at "Saint Joe." After breakfast, I wandered out to say good-by to the stock. The horses were in the back pasture as if they expected the Studebaker to challenge them to a race to the barn. The cows had worked themselves to the same pasture after milking. The pigs were spread out all over the farm rooting or wallowing in the mud by the windmill.

I climbed on top to the farrowing shed and surveyed the south half of the farm. Here was where I caught the piglets for the veterinarian. Down in the south pasture was where the sheep had been. I looked over the garden where the rows of fresh vegetables fed us during the summer and where the supplies for canning would come from. Grandma would be in her bonnet picking peas or beans for supper.

I climbed through the fence and advanced on the calves. They retreated to the farthest corner and eyeballed me. They were getting too big to harass and would soon go to market or to the food locker. Next, I "smugged" around in the car barn with its greasy tools and oily smell. I climbed the Studebaker's running board for the last time. Dad would never let me ride on the Ford's running board.

I checked out the full hay loft where I had discovered the hen and her chicks. I had helped put the hay up there. I put an ear of corn through the sheller, grabbed the bucket and headed for the chicken yard.

The rooster watched me advance on him until I got in his personal space. Then he sidestepped away keeping his eye on me. I flung a handful toward a group of hens. They jumped with surprise and began their "found food" clucking while popping up the kernels. The rooster advanced toward the excited hens with deep, menacing clucks telling them to make way for their master. I placed myself between the rooster and the hens. Every time the rooster tried to get around me, I moved to block him. We kept up the dance until the corn was gone.

The corn game had enticed the laying hens out of their boxes so I collected what eggs had already accumulated and put them in the egg carton. It was almost time for the egg man to come by and pick up the crate. Grandma would get her egg money minus the cost of the laying mash. The feed came in brightly colored sacks which might end up in a quilt or even a dress.

I went into the house and wound up the Victrola. After a few records I wandered over to the glass book case. Nothing would change my sad mood. I settled into one of the porch swings for some violent swinging. Grandma found me there for dinner.

After dinner, I lay down on the cot on the front porch and paged through   for the umteenth time. The pictures of the homeless people and the destroyed buildings always fascinated me, but didn't improve my mood. It was hot and quiet.

This year I had done almost everything. I had watched the oats get combined. Or was it the wheat? So much had happened this summer.

Late in the summer, we had taken a load of hogs to St. Joseph. One morning Charlie Hoit brought his truck to the feedlot. Grandad had penned up the lot the night before when the pigs came to feed. Now we drove them to the loading shoot. They piled on each other as the walls got closer together until they spilled into the truck. They were putting up such a racket that the sows came running to add to the cacophony.

The gate on the truck was fastened securely and Charlie headed off for St. Joe. We went back to change our clothes and climb into the Studebaker. After Bethany it was all concrete thump thump to the big city. Grandad knew right where the stock yards were. By the time we reached them, Charlie had already deposited his load of hogs in one of the hundreds of pens. Grandad and I found his group of confused hogs. A man with a straw hat and a cane was walking through them giving them the eye. Somehow the price was agreed on and the pigs were driven to some scales. Grandad went into an office which overlooked the stock yard. Apparently, he walked out with a check for the hogs. We went into town. Ate lunch. Shopped at a couple of stores. Grandma needed some sewing supplies. Then we drove home. There were a few pigs still left to feed at chore time.

The time when the grain was combined in the south forty was more fun. A couple of combines swept over the field cutting the wheat and spilling out the straw at the back. When a hopper of grain was full, Charlie Hoit came up with his truck with solid sides instead of the cage used for transporting stock and received a squirt of grain. When a truck was full, it left for a grain bin on the farm or a grain elevator and scales and another took its place. There wasn't much I could do but stand around and keep track of the water jug in case someone needed it.

The name combine was derived from the fact that the machine was both a binder and a thresher. Some years earlier I had been on the farm when the threshing crew arrived. Then a separate machine cut the grain and bound the stalks into sheaves with binder twine. Men walked behind the binder stacking the sheaves. The arrival of the threshing crew was another opportunity to serve as water boy. Sheaves of wheat were brought to the thresher, the binder twine cut and the sheaves thrown into the hopper. The straw shot out like the plume behind a fast boat making a straw stack. Again the grain accumulated until a truck came by to pick up the load. Both combining and threshing presented an opportunity for one of those famous farm dinners.

I must have dozed for the sound of a tractor woke me. I watched as one of the Manering girls drove a huge hay baler into the hay field across from the farm house. Soon a team of horses came through pulling a flatbed wagon. The baler started down a windrow. With much banging and clattering, the modern dinosaur took in the hay at one end and deposited compacted bales from the other end. I walked across the road to the fence to get a better look avoiding the poison ivy. It was the first time I had seen a baler working.

The next time Geraldine Manering came by she stopped the tractor. "Hey, Perry, you goen' back to Wisconsin today?"

I nodded. "Can I work on the baler?" I asked.

"Ask your Grandad," she answered and started down the windrow.

"Grandad, Grandad," I cried as I rushed through the front door. "Geraldine asked me to help on the baler." Grandad stopped to think for a minute. Then he walked to the mud porch and slipped on his boots, taking so long to lace them.

At the door he nodded, "Come on." Grandad and I walked past the smoke house, out through the barn yard, through the gate and into the hay field. "You listen to me now, you remember, Pard?"

"Yes," I replied with all the sincerity I could express remembering the swimming pool incident.

The next time the baler came around it stopped at Grandad and me. "Grandad climbed on the tractor wheel and talked with Geraldine. She was wearing one of those things called a halter and her bare back and shoulders were almost black from working in the sun. Grandad climbed down and took me to the side of the baler. "You show the boy here how to feed the baling wire," he told one of the Manering hired hands. I climbed next to him and sat on the board that ran alongside the baling mechanism. When the baler started up the man pushed a long strand of wire into a hole. Somehow the machinery mashed the hay into a rectangular block and rapped two strands of wire around it end to end.

Half way around the field the man motioned me to start feeding the wire. By the tame the baler had come back to where Grandad was standing, I had the routine. I waved at Grandad and he smiled back. The next time around, the man swung off and Grandad swung on. He yelled in my ear over the clanking of the machinery, "You do this as long as you want. I'll come get you when it's time to get dressed for the train."

Grandad's words took the fun out of the baler for a moment. I had almost forgotten this was my last day. Next time around the field, Grandad was missing and the helper was hefting bales onto the flat bed.

All too soon Grandad reappeared waving at Geraldine. She stopped near the flat bed, which by now had four or five rows of bales stacked on, and I climbed off. "Thank you,

Perry, you have a good trip. Bye!" She waved and started down a windrow with the helper feeding the wire. My ears were ringing from the noise of the machinery. I had dust in my hair, in my eyes, in my ears. Real work dust. I swaggered into the front porch like a man and was quickly shooed to the back to get a bath in the galvanized tub. Mom brought kettles of boiling water to heat the water from the pump. Even though the water had been sitting in the sun most of the afternoon, it was still well-water cold.

12

Night Train Home

Now most of the dust had been scrubbed away. I was still blowing some grey stuff out of my nose. I looked acceptably clean in my shorts and tennis shoes. I sat in the rear corner of the Studebaker with Grandma watching the farm disappear. Grandad and Mom sat up front. After what seemed like an hour, we stopped in the middle of farm fields in front of a small red brick building.

Grandad started unloading the suitcases. Was this a train station? Where were the tracks? I entered the station with Mom. While she talked with the station master, I watched the telegraph key as it chattered. The room smelled of old wood, oil and coal smoke. I walked out the back door and found myself on a ledge overlooking a railroad cut. There were twenty or more wooden steps leading down to the rails. The station master was the only person other than my family.

Mom and my grandparents sat in the waiting room. I tried to throw stones across the cut. The telegraph kept up a conversation with itself. A big clock with a white face and Roman numerals hung on a wall. It punctuated the telegraph conversation with a slow click, click. "Hurry up and wait, hurry up and wait."

The station was just a whistle-stop. When the station master put up the signal arm down the track, the train would stop. Otherwise, it would speed on through. Mom had made ticket reservations in McFall some days earlier. Grandad and the station master began carrying the baggage down the steps. Mom gave me the box of food. We all stood in the gravel beside the tracks. I was told to be a good boy several times and assured everyone that I had a good time. Maybe I would see the grandparents at Christmas.

"Whoo, whoo, whoooo," sounded from the left. A steam engine rounded a turn about a mile down the track. "Whooo, hoo," was its last word.

The monster came in fast, so fast I thought it wasn't going to stop. The engine came rumbling past, the bell clanging. Then came the baggage car with men hanging out the top of the doors. Faces flashed by. Brakes began to scream. Half way down the olive brown cars two heads peered out of an opening. As the opening got closer a door flopped open, steps appeared and the two men stopped almost in front of our party. A black man in a white jacket jumped down, put a step on the gravel and began handing up the luggage.

Mom kissed Grandad, Grandma kissed me. I kissed Grandad. Grandma kissed Mom. The man in white helped Mom up the steps. Then I climbed the stairs. A man in a navy blue uniform said, "This way sonny." I looked back to see the floor slam down to cover the stairs and caught a glimpse of an old man and an old woman standing where Grandad and Grandma had been. I waved and they waved back. The train was moving. I ran into the car to see if I could see them. Mom was there waving. I watched them get smaller and disappear around a turn.

The train flashed through green and brown fields. The telegraph polls came by in a continuous stutter. Half of the seats were facing in the direction we were traveling. We had four seats to ourselves. They were covered with a heavy cloth and had a white cloth head rest. Everything smelled like coal.

I staggered to the front of the car and tried out the water cooler. I pulled out a folded cup and pushed the button. A stream of water came out of the wall. The car rocked and swayed. Water sloshed out of the thin paper triangle. It was cold but still tasted like coal. I walked from one end of the car to the other. Nothing to do.

"You want supper," Mom asked. She opened the box of food. There was cold, fried chicken, white bread and butter, tomatoes, and even a peanut butter and jelly sandwich with homemade grape jelly. Some of Grandma's peaches served as dessert. The train raced on through Iowa farm land as we ate.

Sometime before dark the porter, the black man in white, came by to ask, "Do you want your berth made up, Mam?" Mom said yes and we moved to different seats. The porter puled down the upper bunk and put in the partitions. Then he made up the top bunk and the bed with the window. Finally he put up the heavy green curtains. Soon a lower and an upper were ready for occupancy.

Mom got the small suitcase from the porter and laid out my pajamas and tooth brush. I headed toward the men's lounge in the front of the car keeping my legs apart. The swaying of the car wouldn't throw me off balance. In the lounge, men were smoking cigars and talking. The door to the little toilet was open and swinging to the rhythm of the swaying train. A curve threw me into the toilet. All there was in the room was a metal toilet with a wooden seat. When I flushed the toilet I thought I could see the ground racing by underneath. I put on my pajamas and carried my clothes into the lounge.

The washbowls were in the lounge, one each in two of the corners. I was sure the men were watching me brush my teeth. I had to go to the ice water around the corner to get a cup of water. Most of the berths were made up by the time I was finished. The heavy green curtains swayed to the motion of the train. Now which berth was mine?

"Mom," I whispered. Then louder, "Mom?" I wove down the corridor running into Mom coming out of the ladies' lounge in her robe and slippers carrying the small suit case. "What's our number, Mom?"

"Twenty-six. Were you lost?"

I went back to 26, separated the curtains and climbed into the bed on the window side. The heavy green shade had been drawn. I pinched the two fasteners and the shade moved up. It was still light. Farm land rushed by. Horses and cows rased their heads to watch. "Wooo, wooo, wo, wo," the whistle signaled. Pigs ran away from the sound, their ears flapping. I knew they were wuffing that their evening rambles had been disturbed. Mom put the suitcase under the bunk and stored some supplies in a green net stretched across the foot of the bed.

When I was smaller, we had shared an upper bunk. It was fun, but I could hardly sit up and had to use a ladder to get up and down. Worse, I couldn't see out. I enjoyed the scenery rushing by. Soon I fell asleep and Mom closed the blind.

Sometime during the night the train's speed changed. The whistle sounded more frequently and a "Ding, ding, ding," changed to a "Dong. Dong. Dong," as we passed a crossing. I pulled open the edge of the blind to peek out. There were lights, and cars, and buildings. A crossing flashed by with cars backed up, the barriers down, the red lights glowing. The train began to slow. More crossings slid by. Car lights illuminated the window for an instant. The bell on the front of the engine began donging. The brakes began complaining. The train jolted to a stop.

I saw a red brick station with baggage trucks pulled by men in red jackets. The wagons clattered on the brick platform. Passengers were getting on. I heard whispers along the curtained isle. I wished Mom wasn't in the way so I could peek out. The train started wheezing and sputtering. Steam and smoke emerged from various openings. The man in the blue-black suit, the conductor, walked by the window carrying a lantern. Farther down the row of cars, he swung the lantern and yelled, "Boooardd." The engine complained with some bumps and grinds. The conductor swung on the moving train at my car. Bang went the metal floor, slam went the door.

The process of dings and lights repeated itself. Soon we were back into the cradle-like rocking. I fell asleep. Sometimes during the night I heard the sad moan of the whistle stroking the night air followed by the dinging bells at a farmland crossing.

"Miz Treadwell, Miz Treadwell, it's seven, your call." The porter's whisper woke me.

"Thank you," Mom replied.

Mom struggled to wrap her robe around her in the cramped bunk. She slipped out with the suit case. I struggled to get my pajamas off and my clothes on. I headed for the men's lounge. No one was there. I used the toilet, splashed water on my face and returned to number 26. I opened the blind and watched the farm land whiz by. Later, Mom stuck her head in the curtains, "Time for breakfast?"

"Sure!"

We packed the suit case and headed toward the dining car pulling open the heavy doors, hearing the rush and suck of the wind before we pushed open the next door. We went through another Pullman car, then a coach with people still trying to sleep in their seats. Finally, we pushed open the door to the dining car. The car smelled like frying bacon. At the door, a black man in a white uniform led us to a white cloth-covered table with a red flower. Bright silverware, white starched napkins and crystal water glasses were already set. Mom looked at the menu and began writing on an order form.

"You want flapjacks or eggs?"

"Flapjacks."

Mom gave the order to the waiter. Soon he came with coffee for Mom and grapefruit juice for me. Then eggs for Mom and two huge pancakes on which a pad of butter was melting. I poured on hot syrup from a white ceramic pitcher and dug in. The railroad crossings and dinging bells were becoming more frequent.

When we finished breakfast and pushed and pulled our way back to the car, we found our berth had been changed back into seats. The train began slowing down as it rushed through the outskirts of a city. Factories, warehouses, truck yards replaced the farmland and small towns. More and more tracks came to run along side the train. The conductor came through saying, "Chicago, Chicago" in a voice just a little above normal volume.

The train began running through tunnels under streets. Then its bell was dingdonging into the station. The brakes made their final complaint. We collected the small suitcase and headed down the steps. The porter was putting luggage on the bricks. Mom motioned to a black man with a red hat. She pointed to her luggage and said. "Hiawatha." The redcap nodded, collected the luggage and headed toward the station. We followed. We walked past the baggage car and hissing engine. Everyone seemed to be in such a hurry. The redcap crossed tracks and zigzagged around baggage trucks. Finally, he started down an orange-yellow train. He turned and asked for the car number. Then he deposited the luggage in front of another porter. Mom opened her purse and gave the redcap some money. A conductor looked at her ticket and allowed us to board. The porter hefted the luggage on.

We settled in our coach seats. The engine complained for some time before backing the train up. Out in the sunlight the train stopped then jumped forward. Soon we were traveling the in-town speed repeating in reverse the trip to the station. After a while we stopped in Milwaukee. Then farm land and a few more stops. I wandered the length of the train straining to pull open the doors. The club car was on one end the dinner on the other. The rest of the cars were coaches.

When the conductor came through yelling "Stevens Point," I knew I was close to home. I watched for some familiar land mark which would tell me. But it was only when the brakes began to squeal that I knew I was home. "Wausau, Wausau," sang the conductor. "Next stop, Wausau." The coach stopped in front of the station. There was Dad, a pipe sticking out of his face. We carefully went down the steep steps.

"How was your summer?" he asked.

"Fine, fine."

Then Mom and Dad had some catch up conversation to do. The black Ford took this farm boy back to 11th Street. Home appeared so green and overgrown. It was my last Pullman trip. This was the summer of 1941. World War II would begin in December and all the trains would be used for the war effort. After the war it was easier to drive than take the worn out trains much of the time. I am pleased that I can remember the romance of the night train home.

After Words

Grandad and Grandma sold the farm and moved to Long Beach, California in the fall of 1947. Grandma suffered from asthma so badly that her doctor advised either move or die. Mom packed up all the Victrola records and many of the books that I had grown up on. I did lose *The Dark Continent* and *The San Francisco Fire and Earthquake*.

In 1962, I brought my young family back to visit Uncle Ben and Aunt Florence. I had heard that our farmhouse had been burned down for insurance. The road past the farm was now black top. I could not bring myself to walk the land again. I did drive through McFall. A few retired farmers were living there but most of the buildings were also gone.

Grandma lived ten more years in Long Beach. She enjoyed her great grandchildren, and Lawrence Welk and wrestling on the television. Grandad lived five years after her to age 87. They seemed to be quite able to adjust to the rapid change that they had been part of in this century: From listening to the market prices on ear phones to television, from horse travel to jets. Grandad had started a harness business when the automobile was becoming popular. The business failed. Grandmother's father was the first man killed in an automobile accident in Gentry county in 1911.

Nevertheless, the fact that my grandmother's grandfather had a house slave, Venus, cannot be ignored. She was the daughter of Patton house slaves. The fact that she stayed with the Morgan family until her death in 1941 does not excuse slavery or, more so, our attitude toward black people. I don't believe that she was ever considered a member of the family the way an aunt by blood would be. Notice the distance between Venus and the rest of the family in the family picture. Most black people at that time were invisible. Grandad easily sang the Froggie song with "Nigger Man" replacing "little, old man." A brown nut was called a Nigger Toe. He grew up with the word and so did I. My grandparents witnessed the enfranchisement of African-Americans.

I missed hearing them tell about their reaction to the 20th century. Both were in their 20s at the turn of the century. More importantly while growing up I missed my grandfather's Grandfather Stories. Tragically, I only have the Froggie song. When he was alive, I missed my opportunity to push my frontier back into the 19th century. I was too busy to ask him about his boyhood. That is why I have written these memories.